Praise for Dorothea Grossman

"Dorothea Grossman's poetry is funny, wild, and incredibly beautiful. It's a shorthand for what we can't help knowing, even without words, that nature is in us and all around us. 'The surf surrounds like a headache,' over us shines 'the kind moon.' Even breakfast is a cosmic adventure: 'the quiet glow of marmalade,' 'the eye-opening properties of eggs.' We can see just as she says that remembering is 'a form of missing.' The startling jumps in imagination are in her hands only necessary changes in direction. I think of a line or an image, nod, smile, and then, taking it in, am stopped dead in my tracks. How does she do it?"
—Elaine Terranova, poet

"Dottie Grossman is an essentially American poet. In her love lyrics especially, you can often sense the pressure, light as it may be, of American popular music of the 20th century. It's a very American feeling, a kind of ironic romanticism where the adjective, though it may dominate, is never allowed to cancel out the noun."
—Russell Astley, teacher, critic and writer

"Clear, odd, personal, funny or wild-weird, curious and lucid."
—Allen Ginsberg

"Each poem is a compact expression of whimsy and heartbreak."
—David DuPont

The Fun of Speaking English

Selected Poems

The Fun of Speaking English

Selected Poems

Dorothea Grossman

coffeetownpress
Seattle, WA

coffeetownpress

Coffeetown Press
PO Box 70515
Seattle, WA 98127

For more information go to:
www.coffeetownpress.com

Front cover design and illustration by
Benjamin R. Marcus
www.BenjaminRMarcus.com
Back cover design by Sabrina Sun

The Fun of Speaking English: Selected Poems
Copyright © 2012 by Dorothea Grossman

ISBN: 978-1-60381-149-1 (Trade Paper)
ISBN: 978-1-60381-150-7 (eBook)

LOC Control Number: 2012939540

Printed in the United States of America

For Richard, with love

Dear Reader,

As Coffeetown Press was in the final stages of production for *The Fun of Speaking English*, we were saddened to hear of Dorothea Grossman's sudden death on May 6, 2012. She was 74 years old.

Our sadness is somewhat relieved by the knowledge that Dottie told her friends how pleased and happy she was with our collaboration. She had a chance to see and approve every element before she died. We are honored to do our part to ensure that her legacy endures.

For a touching online tribute to Dottie by her close friend, jazz musician Mark Weber, please visit markweber.free-jazz.net.

Sincerely,

Catherine Treadgold
Publisher, Coffeetown Press

Acknowledgments

The following poems appeared in *Poetry Magazine,* March 2010:

"For Allen Ginsberg," "The Two Times I Loved You the Most in a Car," "Noon Concert," "I Knew Something Was Wrong," "I Allow Myself," "Untitled," "It Is Not So Much That I Miss You," "Love Poem."

The following were self-published in *Cuttings: Selected Poems 1978-1988*:

"Morning," "In The Evening," "Dear Terre Haute," "Night: Death Valley," "Yosemite," "Proposal," "Holiday on the Dance Floor," "When It Rains."

The following were self-published in Poems From Cave 17: Selected Poems 1989-1996:

"I Put My Hand," "Ten PM," "Home," "In Mexico," "World War II," "In 1992," "All Day at the Window," "Henny Youngman Told His Landlord."

The following were published in *Take Out #6*, Take Out Press, 2001:

"Even Your Ears" (also appears in liner notes for CD *Richard Grossman Trio: Even Your Ears* hatOLOGY CD 515, 1998), "Drive-By," "Good Friday," "In Cambria," "The El Niño Variations," "The Poetry of Children" (also appeared in *WordWrights #17*).

My thanks to Russell Astley, Doug Benezra, Rob Blakeslee, Phyllis Hatfield, JW Sato, Elaine Terranova, Emily Warn, Laura Winter and Benjamin R. Marcus.

Foreword

As a cranky grad student at SCI-Arc in Santa Monica in the '80s, and, like her, originally from Philadelphia, I bonded quickly with Dottie, who worked part-time in the school office. By the time I left, and partly with her help, I had learned to discern the subtle shifts in light and temperature that Los Angeles life provided, and to stop comparing it to any other city I knew.

With her sardonic outlook, her eschewal of driving, and her unapologetic cigarettes, Dottie might seem at first glance an LA outsider. But to know her at all, and especially to know her through her writing, is to learn how intellect can be sly, and how warmth and optimism need not be confused with superficial "cheerfulness."

Poetry Magazine's Wood Prize and, most recently, the Pushcart Prize nomination were accolades that were less important to Dottie for their prestige than for their signal that her work was being read and enjoyed; that people—specific people—"got it."

After Dottie returned from a gig, she dwelled less on the numbers of people who showed up, than if some listening portion responded with mindful recognition. Only then did she allow herself, cautiously, to bask.

Dottie's concise writing and her dry delivery seem at first a deliberate antidote to both the sunny fluff or plodding "meaningfulness" that passes for modern poetry. But like the art of a few other Southern California transplants, Dottie's is true Los Angeles—deceptively plain, informed by improvisation, and finally, reassuring.

—Benjamin Marcus

Contents

BEFORE

Summer	1
Dear Terre Haute	2
As My Mother Gets Ready to Die	3
Furnishings	4
I Think About You	5
Contrast	6
Home	7
In the Evening	8
For the New Kid	9
Fairy Tale	10
Yosemite	11
Sorry to Disappoint You	12
Rainy Place, Washington	13
Love Poem	14
Maybe a Hummingbird	15
The El Niño Variations	16
Not Exactly Haiku	17
In the Rich Dark Nave	18
North of Here	19
In Cambria	20
Three Sleep Stanzas	21
As the World Turns	23
The Man Who Loves His Job	24
Night, Death Valley	25
Children's Department	26
In 1981, Hurricane Andrew	27
World War II	28
War and Peace	29
Gemstones	30

DURING

I Put My Hand   33
New York Minute   34
Composition   35
For Allen Ginsberg   36
Map of the United States   37
The Poetry of Children   38
Drive-By   39
Your Shirts   41
April, 2003   42
When I Think About You   43
Untitled   44
Love Poem #2   45
Future Past   46
The Museum of Rain   47
Prime Time   48
Daria   49
Proposal   51
All Day   52
Definition of Happiness #5013   53

NOW

In Mexico   57
Indian Summer, Where I Live   58
Even Your Ears   59
Commercial Break   60
I Have Put   61
Wind Shift   62
The Two Times I Loved You the Most in a Car   63
Holiday   65
Message in a Bottle   66
Noon Concert   67

The First Time I Ate Sushi   68
I Knew...   69
It Is Not So Much That I Miss You   70
Story   71
Grade School   72
For The Newly-Bereaved   73
Two Reasons Why I Like Men   74
Mendocino Coast, 1967   75
Lists   76
I Allow Myself   77
The Opposite of Brazil   78
EKG   79
Summer: Three Ways   80
Not Again   82

THE HENNY YOUNGMAN POEMS

Henny Youngman's New Year's Resolution   85
Henny Youngman Told His Landlord   86
Henny Youngman's Feng Shui   87
On the Dance Floor   88
Capitalism   89
If You Love Him Enough   90
When You Get to Chartres   91
At the Bookstore   92
Henny Youngman's Music   93
Global Warming   94
Henny Youngman Says   95
Henny Youngman's Secret   96
When It Rains   97
NOTES   99

BEFORE

Summer

Driving through gangs

of radios and insects;

the air still hot tonight

smelling of burnt toast

and wet trees,

I taste the soft pink fruit

of August upon August.

The stars are old and mysterious,

like cave paintings

by wild men

without a word for *summer.*

Dear Terre Haute

Last night I

dreamed about you,

although I haven't

thought of you

for years.

So much has happened

since I saw you:

I grew up,

found out

about Wyoming,

and stopped smoking.

Are you still

on the right bank

of the Mississippi?

As My Mother Gets Ready to Die

The silent TV

presides like a priest

in this room

full of her medicines

and fingerprints.

On-screen, a woman talks to a tarantula

that climbs onto her palm

and stretches its legs

like a velvet umbrella.

Furnishings

Afternoon green sofa

in tumbled sunlight:

just for this minute,

we are a tableau of happiness;

good time-binders, making history

with words and music,

but a little self-conscious,

wishing to keep it to ourselves,

play it back, re-string and polish it

so it stays

in this room of green sofa,

mantel with no clock,

cold fireplace because

it is still summer.

I Think About You

I think about you driving home

along roads as romantic as dreams

fortified by a night on the town.

You probably see stars

through a tangle of trees,

like that picture by Georgia O'Keeffe.

I think about you driving home

in a downpour,

when the wind, drunk with eucalyptus,

hums when it hits you.

Contrast

I bought myself

A New York–colored scarf;

Gray, with a dash of

Fire-engine red,

And not exactly noisy,

But--you know--busy.

Home

Is where we

love each other

and where we

come to look things up.

Everything else

is Away.

In the Evening

Watering the garden,

listening to the classics,

you are rich

in nosegays and ceramics.

This afternoon

your tailored white arm

adjusting the rear-view mirror

reproached the sun.

You have been

important and beautiful

ever since

your fruit-tinged

morning.

For the New Kid

I hope you will always be warm,

and jumping-jack happy.

I can't wait to show you those days

when the mountains repeat themselves

slowly

as blue after blue after blue.

Fairy Tale

There was a time

(please, God, not that long ago),

I wanted to run away

and join the circus.

It seemed realistic:

the clowns would feed me,

I would get to know the sky

in different places,

and the lions would understand

that I was on their side.

Yosemite

Gasping in the hot

valley twilight,

you remember the chilly

higher elevations

where ancient trees

grow feminine at midnight:

dizzy with stars,

tottering on

big, soft feet.

Sorry to Disappoint You

As the elder in your Chinese house,

I have almost no wisdom to offer:

A few books, a few poems –

I'm not sure there's anything else,

except that I once shook John Coltrane's
hand,

and sex in the morning is more fun

than cereal.

The rest you already know.

Rainy Place, Washington

Even the children

were covered with moss,

like little trees,

sucking what daylight

was left

after the rivers,

the mountains,

the bridges

were finished.

Love Poem

In a lightning bolt

of memory,

I see our statue of Buddha

(a wedding gift from Uncle Gene)

which always sat

on top of the speaker cabinet.

When a visitor asked,

"So, does Buddha like jazz?"

you said, "I hope so.

He's been getting it up the ass

for a long time."

Maybe a Hummingbird

Just before I killed that bug,

I had the guilty thought

that it might be you,

reincarnated,

but I told myself

that if you did return,

it would be as a much

higher life form;

maybe a hummingbird.

DOROTHEA GROSSMAN

The El Niño Variations

Maybe because it's not raining today

(El Niño is drunk or asleep),

I'm more vulnerable than usual,

riding the Number Eight Bus

down Ocean Park Boulevard,

thinking about my debt

to American poets,

hearing Ginsberg's voice

testing my cadences.

We pass by the yellow house,

and the shadows come out

like débutantes

into this bushy-tailed morning.

Not Exactly Haiku

Gray monster of a ship

on the horizon –

you would have said,

"Look at that!"

Red maple trees

in the fog,

and two widows

on their gray–haired walk.

In the Rich Dark Nave

In the rich dark nave of you,

I close my eyes and taste sunlight.

It's not that you're holy,

but there's more life in your shadow

than in all of blazing Easter.

North of Here

In the canyons below

the spinach-flecked hills

I stick wildflowers

into sky-colored bottles

for my imaginary cottage.

I could impress you

with made-up tales

about a flower seller

from Japan;

you could

imagine me comparing

the white buds of Topanga

to the pink sprays

of Osaka.

In Cambria

Sugar-snap peas

at the Farmers' Market;

the rest of the day is colorless.

We're looking for a back road

with real cows and berries.

The beach goes on and on and on,

like television.

Three Sleep Stanzas

In a sleep

ruffled by guilt

I dream of my family

praying together,

childishly.

They are so small

that I suddenly understand

their common nightmare

and why they call themselves

by one name.

In the dream

of skyscrapers

as paper dolls

each has its wardrobe

of tenants

that can be moved

around forever.

In recurring Cary Grant

Dream Number One,

he appears on Christmas Evening

to bless the animals.

Morning

Walking past the mental hospital

I smell coffee brewing,

and picture the muttering madmen

measuring and pouring,

preparing for

another perfect landing.

As the World Turns

The Cape Chestnuts

are on their way out;

soon, in the towns

with the Indian names

there will be

Christmas trees

instead of pumpkins,

and the wind

that scooped

the quilted desert

into a harvest bouquet

will invent

something new.

The Man Who Loves His Job

"You can smell

the pumper truck

before you see it,

on the days when

concrete gets poured.

(Did you know

colored concrete

smells different?)

We all stand around,

eating huevos rancheros,

and trying not

to look happy."

Night, Death Valley

Radio music

was never so welcome

as in this chalky air

among the shooting stars

and flying saucers.

Children's Department

The library always smells

like this:

an ancient stew

of vinegar and wood.

It's autumn, again,

and I can do anything.

In 1981, Hurricane Andrew

Recalls My Aunt's First Hurricane, 50 Years Ago, in
New Jersey

"There was Mike

in a white suit,

jumping over the hot wires

to get to me.

The waves were so high,

you couldn't tell

where the sky ended."

World War II

I love you

as if it's World War II

and you've just been "called up."

It's raining hard,

and I'm wearing a sensational goodbye
hat.

War and Peace

You can tell

the war is over

by the choke hold

of roses and bougainvillea

in the alleys.

I bend my 50-year-old neck

to see the crossed swords

of the 30-foot bamboo grove.

At rush hour:

pigeon-wing sky

and hibiscus

the color of murder.

Gemstones

Today I bought

the first pumpkin

of my season.

The sun was

hitting the water

in tiny explosions;

the grass was as pure

as a revival meeting.

I thought of your smile

on my long walk home

with the leaves dropping aimlessly

and the rasp

of roller skates.

When the door opened

you burst upon me

like a diamond.

DURING

I Put My Hand

I put my hand

up your sleeve,

looking for

God-knows-what

and your arm seems

protected and holy.

I feel unworthy,

the way I sometimes do

around fresh vegetables.

DOROTHEA GROSSMAN

New York Minute

The rain surprised us

and of course, all the taxis

dried up and disappeared.

We settled for one of those

glassy hotels

with clean restrooms and

a piano bar

cozily serving up hors d'oeuvres

and standards,

like "Violets For Your Furs"

and "September In The Rain."

I think we were drinking Manhattans,

more as a salute to the moment

than anything else

because we were sophisticated,

but not yet romantic.

Romantic came later.

Composition

This is as pure as it gets –

a chunk of bottle–blue sky

in the doorway,

5:30 a.m., all summer.

Two minutes of unadulterated truth,

followed by crowd–pleasing dawn.

For Allen Ginsberg

Among other things,

thanks for explaining

how the generous death

of old trees

forms

the red powdered floor

of the forest.

Map of the United States

I don't think I have ever been in one of
the pink states,

but I have been in Kansas, which is green

and Nebraska, which is orange,

and barely sampled the blue Texas
Panhandle.

I've spent most of my time in the yellow
ones.

DOROTHEA GROSSMAN

The Poetry of Children

is that they just got here,

so they're still smooth

as river rocks.

In those honey-dipped days,

I was always on the verge

of drowning in you;

ending up like

a spider in amber.

Not a bad way to go,

come to think of it;

suspended for all time

in clear fossil Jello.

Good Friday, and a poem

comes barging in

like a drunk,

wearing Christ-colored nail polish.

Drive-By

A flowered chintz couch

appeared at the curb,

like a peace offering.

I came home to a sky

that was moving

in waltz time –

like lace,

causing big, random shadows

on hills

that were already gold,

even though it was

still much too soon

to be summer.

November overtook me

like a sweater:

first, that moment of panic

when I pulled it over my head,

and then the light.

Your Shirts

I'd forgotten how I used to love your shirts,

till I saw one that made me remember.

I could have hugged the man who wore it,

to see if he smiled or smelled like you

that day you got back from Minnesota

with a postcard of Billy the Kid,

who looked (come to think of it) cross-eyed,

like most men in early American photos.

April, 2003

Three years and four months

into this new century,

my head is full of numbers.

A string quartet plays a string quartet

while sunshine follows me downstairs.

Today, I like things the way they are.

When I Think About You

When I think about you

I can feel my wings beating.

There's enough love in your voice

to make me fly.

DOROTHEA GROSSMAN

Untitled

"I don't own an exquisite way to
move around in the night."
—Doug Benezra, 9/18/05

It occurs to me that,

when I die,

they might find the necklace

I dropped behind the bed

and wonder

how long it was there,

and whether I'd missed it.

But will they care

about my favorite color,

my long-range plans,

or my habit of searching myself

for signs of rust?

Love Poem #2

When you wake up

you smile,

as if you'd swum

with dolphins

and learned

their secrets,

or been someplace

forbidden,

where the women

wear silk

the colors of water.

Future Past

If I had stayed asleep

I would have missed

the fun of speaking English,

the quiet satisfaction

of appointments kept,

the way dreams change

when you try to describe them.

The Museum of Rain

collects kingdoms and corpses

and rivers of newly sprung flowers,

in addition to samples

of grass under glass

and statues of soaking wet lovers.

Prime Time

Thirteen days since I visited the
supermarket;

the magazines in my bathroom are no
longer relevant.

It was Daylight Savings Time the last time I
dusted;

the air conditioner was running

and the plants needed water.

I got my hair cut last week;

it's time for my six-month dental checkup.

All day, every day, I look at your
photograph

in changing lights and shadows

(think of Cezanne, eternally

painting his mountain).

Your face is the only reliable way

I tell time anymore.

Daria

This is Daria:

she's five years old,

with pale hair that swings,

and serious glasses.

She shook my hand

when we were introduced,

and said "I have another

friend named Dottie,

and her knee hurts."

Last night, I rode the dark dream trolley

to ten years old.

Downtown department stores

were only open late

on Wednesdays,

except during Christmas.

On the west coast,

Schoenberg was still alive,

playing a game of chess;

the Santa Ana winds

were creaking

and the sky was that Crayola

navy blue I never saw

in any season

until this.

Proposal

I would paint wild flowers

that never grow

in this man's land

and heap them on you

clumsily.

They should be

blurry purple or chartreuse

and scatter dots of light as randomly

as windows in the dusk

on unsafe roads.

All Day

All day,

at the window,

I sit next to the weather,

studying shadows

like an indoor cat,

until dusk,

when the sky

walks me home.

Definition of Happiness #5013

They're playing Johnny Mercer

on the radio

there's a bowl of yellow apples

on the table,

you just came in, whistling,

and tomorrow's a national holiday.

NOW

In Mexico

We waited the storm out

under a tree in Mexico.

The hills were crawling

with wild mustard.

In the rain,

the dogs and the streets

ran yellow.

DOROTHEA GROSSMAN

Indian Summer, Where I Live

Season of flutes

and bare arms,

the ruckus of bees

at the door,

snarl of fire engines

in this desert.

I am already thinking

of pumpkins and silence,

the homecoming of color,

the rescue of first rain.

Even Your Ears

I have to tell you

there are times

when the sun strikes me

like a gong,

and I remember everything,

even your ears.

Commercial Break

This sunset is being brought to you

by smog,

which has basted the air

to a breathtaking orange

shot through

with robin's-egg blue.

I Have Put

I have put my little house to bed.

Here, everything has its own place,

its own rhythm,

like a still life.

So the apples go here,

and the lemons

a little to the left.

Wind Shift

I felt the wind shift last night,

lawless and wild,

like lions,

like fire,

like decisions made

deep,

before language.

The Two Times I Loved You the Most in a Car

It was your idea

to park and watch the elephants

swaying among the trees

like royalty

at that make-believe safari

near Laguna.

I didn't know anything that big

could be so quiet.

And once, you stopped

on a dark desert road,

to show me the stars

climbing over each other

riotously

like insects;

like an orchestra

thrashing its way

through time itself.

I never saw light that way

again.

Holiday

Now that I can afford

the luxury of dreams again,

they burst around my head

like firecrackers.

All day I must be

wearing the debris

of last night's happy

Chinese New Year.

DOROTHEA GROSSMAN

Message in a Bottle

Remember that time

I was washing the dishes

and you were in the next room

and you ran into the kitchen

when a bubble of detergent

landed on you

and you thought

I sent it on purpose

like a blown kiss,

to tell you I loved you?

Noon Concert

These frail, white widows

who get their hair done weekly

in tight curls,

like little flowers

bend their heads

until the applause

says it's time

to be brave, again.

DOROTHEA GROSSMAN

The First Time I Ate Sushi

Loving you

feels religious,

like the first time

I ate sushi.

I Knew...

I knew something was wrong

the day I tried to pick up a

small piece of sunlight

and it slithered through my fingers,

not wanting to take shape.

Everything else stayed the same –

the chairs and the carpet

and all the corners

where the waiting continued.

It Is Not So Much That I Miss You

It is not so much that I miss you

as the remembering

which I suppose is a form of missing

except more positive,

like the time of the blackout

when fear was my first response

followed by love of the dark.

Story

The way I miss you

in the rain

is like the story

about the kid

who loves his father

so much

he wants to marry him.

DOROTHEA GROSSMAN

Grade School

The expectation was

that I could recognize

a sycamore tree's

splotchy bark

in my black and white world,

but it was not so.

I only knew the words

"tree" and "house"

and I hoped they

would teach me

the rest.

For The Newly-Bereaved

It doesn't matter

whether you open the door,

turn on the music

or stand up.

All you really have to do

is feed the cat.

Two Reasons Why I Like Men

The vulnerability of their legs

in shorts,

The innocence of their bare chests

in August.

Mendocino Coast, 1967

Inland, where the grasses and grapes
lived,

we could not have imagined

the rocks, the cold clouds –

the surf that would surround us

like a headache,

and those long tubes of kelp

like noodles

from another world

where, with the music of foghorns

and wind chimes,

even the kind moon

seemed dangerous.

DOROTHEA GROSSMAN

Lists

"You have to have time to feel sorry for yourself if
you want to be a good abstract expressionist."
– Robert Rauschenberg

She read her long poem that listed

just about everything in the world.

Afterwards, I told her,

"Thanks, you saved me the trouble."

And, talking about poetry,

Billy Collins (our ex-Poet Laureate) says,

... "how will it ever end?

Unless the day finally arrives

when we have compared everything in
the world

to everything else in the world."

My sentiments, exactly.

I Allow Myself

I allow myself

the luxury of breakfast

(I am no nun, for Christ's sake).

Charmed as I am

by the sputter of bacon

and the eye–opening properties

of eggs,

it's the coffee

that's really sacramental.

In the old days,

I spread fires and floods and pestilence

on my toast.

Nowadays, I'm more selective,

I only read my horoscope

by the quiet glow of the marmalade.

The Opposite of Brazil

On cloudy days at the beach

no illusions – not even one palm tree –

can happen.

Think of beige

or the sobriety of linen.

EKG

That's my heart,

sloshing around

senselessly

in what sounds like

a big metal bucket

that holds

lots of cold beers

for a party.

DOROTHEA GROSSMAN

Summer: Three Ways

I've been learning English

all my life,

so I'm pretty good at it,

but every summer brings

my throat and brain

new challenges.

Here, where rain is so rare,

I've lost my sense of smell,

but late at night,

under a sheen of oil

that feels very much like rain,

the city tastes like fish.

Sometimes, in my green retreat,

the weather makes a joke,

with early falling leaves

and snowy flowers.

It's August;

nothing will change

until we tell it to.

Not Again

As if I needed

another reminder

of you

in winter,

when the lights dance

on the bridges

and a tune on the piano

draws blood.

You have invaded

my small country

expertly,

like a bullet.

THE HENNY YOUNGMAN POEMS

(selections from an ongoing series in tribute to the
late comedian)

Henny Youngman's
New Year's Resolution

I'll only eat food

prepared by

people who love me.

Henny Youngman
Told His Landlord

Henny Youngman told his landlord,

"Send somebody up here right away;

my cat has stopped purring."

Henny Youngman's Feng Shui

When advised of the positive *chi*

that a water element would bring

to the southwest corner of his bedroom,

Henny Youngman instantly

moved the dog's water dish.

On the Dance Floor

On the dance floor

he's no Fred Astaire,

but he's a pretty good

Henny Youngman.

Capitalism

Henny Youngman can't find an investor

for his latest business venture:

a franchise he calls

The No Vacancy Motel.

If You Love Him Enough

If you love him enough,

Henny Youngman will give you

whatever you want, plus expenses.

When You Get to Chartres

When you get to Chartres

be sure and catch

the Henny Youngman Cathedral.

DOROTHEA GROSSMAN

At the Bookstore

At the bookstore,

Henny Youngman tells the sales clerk,

"I'm in a hurry,

so I'll just have some haiku."

Henny Youngman's Music

Henny Youngman's music

for the millennium

is his Suite for Teenager and Orchestra.

Global Warming

When he got an invitation

to the Global Warming Summit,

Henny Youngman volunteered

to bring the salad.

Henny Youngman Says

Henny Youngman says,

"To hell with peace,

let's give Yoko Ono a chance."

Henny Youngman's Secret

When you know

Henny Youngman

really well

you'll find out

where he keeps

his ruby slippers.

When It Rains

When it rains in Los Angeles

they say Henny Youngman is crying.

NOTES

1. Henry "Henny" Youngman (March 16, 1906 – February 24, 1998) was a British-born American comedian and violinist famous for one-liners—short, simple jokes usually delivered rapid-fire. His best known one-liner was "Take my wife...please". His stand-up style was popular at what were known as Borscht Belt hotels, bungalow colonies and summer camps in upper New York State, which were mostly frequented by Jewish New Yorkers from the 1920s through the 1960s.

CPSIA information can be obtained
at www.ICGtesting.com
Printed in the USA
LVHW030215200821
695686LV00006B/891

9 781603 811491